I0426054

June 2012

INTELLIGENCE COMMUNITY PERSONNEL

Strategic Approach and Training Requirements Needed to Guide Joint Duty Program

June 2012

INTELLIGENCE COMMUNITY PERSONNEL

Strategic Approach and Training Requirements Needed to Guide Joint Duty Program

Why GAO Did This Study

In the years following the terrorist attacks on September 11, 2001, Congress enacted the Intelligence Reform and Terrorism Prevention Act of 2004, which gives the Director of National Intelligence the responsibility to establish a personnel rotational program (the Joint Duty Program) across the IC. The intended purpose is to facilitate IC personnel's understanding of the wide range of intelligence requirements, methods, users, and capabilities. GAO evaluated the extent to which (1) IC elements are participating in the Joint Duty Program, (2) the ODNI has developed a strategic framework to help ensure the effective implementation of the Joint Duty Program, and (3) ODNI has established training and education programs to support the Joint Duty Program. GAO reviewed the Joint Duty Program's legislative requirements and guidance, analyzed data on program participants, and interviewed program officials from the entire IC.

What GAO Recommends

GAO recommends that DHS take steps to have the Coast Guard participate in the Joint Duty Program. GAO also recommends that ODNI develop a strategic framework to implement the program across the IC and that ODNI establish and document the program's training requirements and develop a plan and timeline for implementing them. DHS and the Coast Guard agreed with GAO's recommendation to the Coast Guard. ODNI generally agreed with GAO's recommendations, but raised concerns about the findings on performance goals and the strategic framework. GAO continues to believe in the findings as stated in the report.

View GAO-12-679. For more information, contact Brenda S. Farrell, (202) 512-3604 or farrellb@gao.gov.

What GAO Found

All of the Intelligence Community (IC) elements except for one are participating in the Joint Duty Program and the IC elements generally view the program as beneficial. The Office of the Director of National Intelligence (ODNI), the Defense Security Service, the Office of the Under Secretary of Defense for Intelligence, and 15 other IC components have identified an office or individual responsible for facilitating the program. However, the U.S. Coast Guard (Coast Guard), which ordinarily operates under the Department of Homeland Security (DHS), does not participate in the program, even though the Intelligence Reform and Terrorism Prevention Act of 2004 and IC guidance stipulate that the Joint Duty Program applies to the defined IC, which includes the Coast Guard's civilian personnel in its National Intelligence Element. Coast Guard officials stated it delayed its participation in the program because it first plans to conduct a workforce study that will determine how the Coast Guard will participate, but it has not identified a timeframe for the study's completion, and the position assigned to conduct the study is currently vacant. As a result, personnel in other IC elements may not fully understand the Coast Guard's intelligence mission and Coast Guard employees may have limited opportunities to collaborate with other IC elements.

ODNI has not established a strategic framework to guide the implementation of the Joint Duty Program across the IC. GAO has noted in prior work the importance of having a strategic framework to guide program implementation. However, ODNI has not clearly defined the program's mission, established performance goals, and measured progress toward achieving those goals. Further, program officials told GAO that they collected IC element data on joint duty rotations, but GAO found that they had not used these data to evaluate progress toward achieving program goals. In addition, although the Director of National Intelligence has emphasized the importance of the program, GAO found that the ODNI Joint Duty Program Office Chief position has experienced repeated turnover since the program's inception. Specifically, five different people have served in the Joint Duty Program Chief position in the past 3 years. Further, ODNI officials stated that the Joint Duty Chief position had recently been downgraded from a Senior National Intelligence Service position to a General Schedule 15 position. Absent a comprehensive strategic framework that transcends turnovers in program leadership, program efforts are disjointed, and decision makers within ODNI lack the information they need to successfully manage the program.

ODNI also has not formally established professional training and education programs to support the Joint Duty Program, as directed in 2007 ODNI guidance. ODNI has identified three IC-related courses intended for personnel participating in the Joint Duty Program but has waived the requirement to complete these courses. Officials from nine IC elements expressed various concerns about the content and rigor of the three courses, such as that the courses could be duplicative of existing agency-specific training courses. Further, ODNI has not yet determined or documented the program's training requirements in guidance and has not yet developed a plan and timeline for implementing the training. As a result, ODNI is not positioned to use the Joint Duty Program to foster the widest possible understanding of intelligence requirements, methods, users, and capabilities.

_____ **United States Government Accountability Office**

Contents

Abbreviations

DOD	Department of Defense
GS	General Schedule
IC	Intelligence Community
IRTPA	Intelligence Reform and Terrorism Prevention Act of 2004
ODNI	Office of the Director of National Intelligence

June 20, 2012

The Honorable Daniel Akaka
Chairman
Subcommittee on Oversight of Management, the Federal Workforce, and
    the District of Columbia
Committee on Homeland Security and Governmental Affairs
United States Senate

The Honorable Jason Chaffetz
Chairman
The Honorable John Tierney
Ranking Member
Subcommittee on National Security, Homeland Defense, and Foreign
    Operations
Committee on Oversight and Government Reform
House of Representatives

The Honorable Jeff Flake
House of Representatives

In the years following the terrorist attacks on September 11, 2001, the
President and Congress commissioned reviews that identified significant
institutional, cultural, and organizational factors that had prevented the
components of the U.S. Intelligence Community[1] (IC) from operating in an
effective and collaborative manner.[2] In one report to the President, a

---

[1]The U.S. Intelligence Community comprises 17 components. The Office of the Director of
National Intelligence oversees the Intelligence Community, and is counted as one of the
17 components. The other 16 components are: the National Security Agency, National
Geospatial-Intelligence Agency, National Reconnaissance Office, Defense Intelligence
Agency, Army Intelligence, Navy Intelligence, Marine Corps Intelligence, Air Force
Intelligence (Air Force Intelligence, Surveillance, and Reconnaissance), Central
Intelligence Agency, Department of Homeland Security (Office of Intelligence and
Analysis), Department of State (Bureau of Intelligence and Research), Department of
Treasury (Office of Intelligence and Analysis), Federal Bureau of Investigation (National
Security Branch), Drug Enforcement Administration (Office of National Security
Intelligence), U.S. Coast Guard (Intelligence and Criminal Investigations), and Department
of Energy (Office of Intelligence and Counterintelligence).

[2]Office of the Director of National Intelligence, *United States Intelligence Community
Report on IC Pay Modernization. Response to Section 308 of H.R. 2082, the Intelligence
Authorization Act for Fiscal Year 2008* (Apr. 22, 2008).

commission concluded that the IC had failed to encourage joint personnel assignments that could break down cultural barriers and foster collaboration among intelligence components.[3] In enacting the Intelligence Reform and Terrorism Prevention Act of 2004 (IRTPA), Congress included a provision requiring the Director of National Intelligence to prescribe mechanisms to facilitate the rotation of IC personnel to other IC elements[4] during their careers, in order to obtain the widest possible understanding of the range of intelligence requirements, methods, users, and capabilities through the IC.[5] Specifically, according to IRTPA, the Director of National Intelligence, in consultation with IC element heads, is to prescribe personnel policies and programs to:

- Encourage and facilitate assignments and details of personnel to national intelligence centers, and between elements of the IC;
- Set standards for education, training, and career development of personnel within the IC; and
- Make service in more than one element of the IC a condition of promotion to such positions within the IC as the Director of National Intelligence specifies.

The Director of National Intelligence issued a directive[6] and policy guidance[7] for the Intelligence Community Civilian Joint Duty Program (Joint Duty Program) in 2006 and 2007, respectively, that prescribe

---

[3]The Commission on the Intelligence Capabilities of the United States Regarding Weapons of Mass Destruction, *Report to the President of the United States* (Mar. 31, 2005).

[4]For purposes of this report, references to the IC elements include the Office of the Under Secretary of Defense for Intelligence, the Defense Security Service, and the 17 IC components noted above because they are all subject to the Joint Duty Program requirement. Although the Defense Security Service is technically not part of the IC, it is also included in our scope because Defense Security Service civilian personnel fall under the Under Secretary for Defense for Intelligence and are subject to the Joint Duty Program requirement.

[5]Pub. L. No. 108-458, § 1011 (2004) (amending § 102A of the National Security Act of 1947, as codified at 50 U.S.C. § 403-1).

[6]Intelligence Community Directive 601, *Human Capital: Joint Intelligence Community Duty Assignments* (May 16, 2006) (as amended Sept. 4, 2009).

[7]Intelligence Community Policy Guidance 601.1, *Intelligence Community Civilian Joint Duty Program Implementing Instructions* (June 25, 2007) (as amended Sept. 4, 2009).

GAO-12-679 Intelligence Community Personnel

requirements for obtaining joint duty credit.[8] According to the directive, IC joint duty positions are typically limited to those classified at General Schedule (GS) 13 and above (or similar categories). A joint duty assignment means a temporary detail of employees away from their home elements to rotational assignments in an appropriate joint duty position with another IC element for at least 12 months.[9] Further, the policy guidance establishes an expectation that ODNI will, in consultation with the heads of the IC elements, develop a Joint Leadership Development Program to provide professional training and education to personnel who are on, or have completed, one or more joint duty assignments. Subject to the provisions of the policy guidance, promotion to Senior Executive/Senior Professional positions is contingent on earning joint duty credit.[10]

In 2009, the Chairman and then-Ranking Member of the Senate Committee on Homeland Security and Governmental Affairs, Subcommittee on Oversight of Government Management, the Federal Workforce, and the District of Columbia, asked us to review the Joint Duty Program. Subsequently, the then-Chairman and then-Ranking Member of the House Committee on Oversight and Government Reform, Subcommittee on National Security and Foreign Affairs, asked to be added as requestors.[11] In response to this request, we examined the

---

[8]Subject to the conditions described in the policy guidance, joint duty credit can generally be earned by working for at least 12 months in another IC element, in an organization outside the IC, within an employee's home element in a position that has been specifically designated as providing joint duty credit, and in certain liaison and equivalent positions or on internal assignments (e.g., serving on joint task forces). Furthermore, any individual deployed to a designated combat zone for 179 days or more will satisfy the 12-month minimum requirement for joint duty credit.

[9]Under the directive, a joint duty assignment may also be a permanent assignment of an employee from a position in one IC element to a position in another IC element.

[10]Under this directive, Senior Executives/Senior Professionals include IC civilian employees in Senior National Intelligence Service, Defense Intelligence Senior Executive Service, Senior Intelligence Service, Senior Executive Service, Senior Level, senior Scientific and Technical, and/or equivalent positions that are classified above GS-15, or employees with comparable rank.

[11]When the 112th Congress organized, the name of the House subcommittee was changed to the Subcommittee on National Security, Homeland Defense, and Foreign Operations. In addition, former Ranking Member Flake was no longer a member of the subcommittee but asked to remain a requester for this engagement, and the new subcommittee Chairman, Representative Chaffetz, asked to be added to the request.

extent to which (1) IC elements are participating in the Joint Duty Program, (2) the Office of the Director of National Intelligence (ODNI) has developed a strategic framework to help ensure the effective implementation of the Joint Duty Program across the IC, and (3) ODNI has established training and education programs to support the Joint Duty Program.

To evaluate the extent to which the IC elements are participating in the Joint Duty Program, we interviewed cognizant agency officials and reviewed program documentation and guidance from ODNI, the Office of the Under Secretary of Defense for Intelligence, the Defense Security Service, and the Joint Duty Program offices (or equivalent entity) from each of the remaining 16 IC components. To evaluate the extent to which ODNI has developed a strategic framework to help ensure the effective implementation of the Joint Duty Program across the IC, we reviewed legislative requirements set out in IRTPA and governmentwide best practices for program implementation;[12] collected, reviewed, and analyzed key guidance issued by ODNI; and interviewed cognizant agency officials within ODNI, the Office of the Under Secretary of Defense for Intelligence, the Defense Security Service, and the joint duty program offices (or similar entity) of each of the remaining 16 IC components. We also requested, reviewed, and analyzed data from the IC elements to describe personnel participation in the IC Joint Duty Program. These data included the job series of individuals on rotations to IC elements and the method by which joint duty credit was earned. We found the data were sufficiently reliable to ascertain the characteristics of IC personnel participating in the Joint Duty Program in fiscal years 2010 and 2011. To evaluate the extent to which ODNI has established training and education programs to support the Joint Duty Program, we reviewed requirements related to training and education programs set out in IRTPA, Intelligence Community Directive 601 and Intelligence Community Policy Guidance 601.1—which prescribe the Joint Duty Program—and analyzed ODNI documents related to those programs. We also interviewed officials from each of the IC elements to gain their perspectives on the actions ODNI had taken to establish training and education requirements for the Joint Duty Program. Additionally, we

---

[12]GAO, *Government Performance: GPRA Modernization Act Provides Opportunities to Help Address Fiscal, Performance, and Management Challenges,* GAO-11-466T (Washington, D.C.: Mar. 16, 2011).

interviewed officials from the National Intelligence University to ascertain the extent to which they support the Joint Duty Program.

We conducted this performance audit from January 2010[13] through June 2012 in accordance with generally accepted government auditing standards. Those standards require that we plan and perform the audit to obtain sufficient, appropriate evidence to provide a reasonable basis for our findings and conclusions based on our audit objectives. We believe that the evidence obtained provides a reasonable basis for our findings and conclusions based on our audit objectives. A more thorough description of our scope and methodology is provided in appendix I.

Background

Organization of the IC

Established by IRTPA, the Director of National Intelligence serves as head of the IC, acts as the principal advisor to the President and National Security Council on intelligence matters, and oversees and directs the implementation of the National Intelligence Program. The IC comprises 17 different organizations across the federal government. The Office of the Under Secretary of Defense for Intelligence oversees all DOD intelligence policies and activities. As shown in figure 1, the IC elements that are subject to ODNI's Joint Duty Program requirements consist of the Office of the Director of National Intelligence, the Office of the Under Secretary of Defense for Intelligence, the Defense Security Service, and 16 IC components.

---

[13]We initially began this engagement in January 2010, and notified ODNI of our intention to schedule an entrance conference in early February. At the end of March 2010, ODNI provided us with a copy of the ODNI Office of the Inspector General, *The Intelligence Community Civilian Joint Duty Program: Implementation Status Report,* CAS-2008-0003 (Washington, D.C.: October 2009). We initially agreed with ODNI to postpone the entrance conference pending our review of their report. Subsequently, section 348 of the Intelligence Authorization Act for Fiscal Year 2010, Pub. L. No. 111-259 (2010), directed ODNI, in consultation with the Comptroller General, to develop a written directive governing GAO's access to information from elements of the IC. Pending issuance of this guidance, we suspended this engagement temporarily. The ODNI issued guidance in April 2011, accompanied by comments from the Comptroller General, and work on this engagement resumed in August 2011. See *Intelligence Community Directive 114: Comptroller General Access to Intelligence Community Information* (effective June 30, 2011).

Figure 1: Organization of the Intelligence Community (IC)

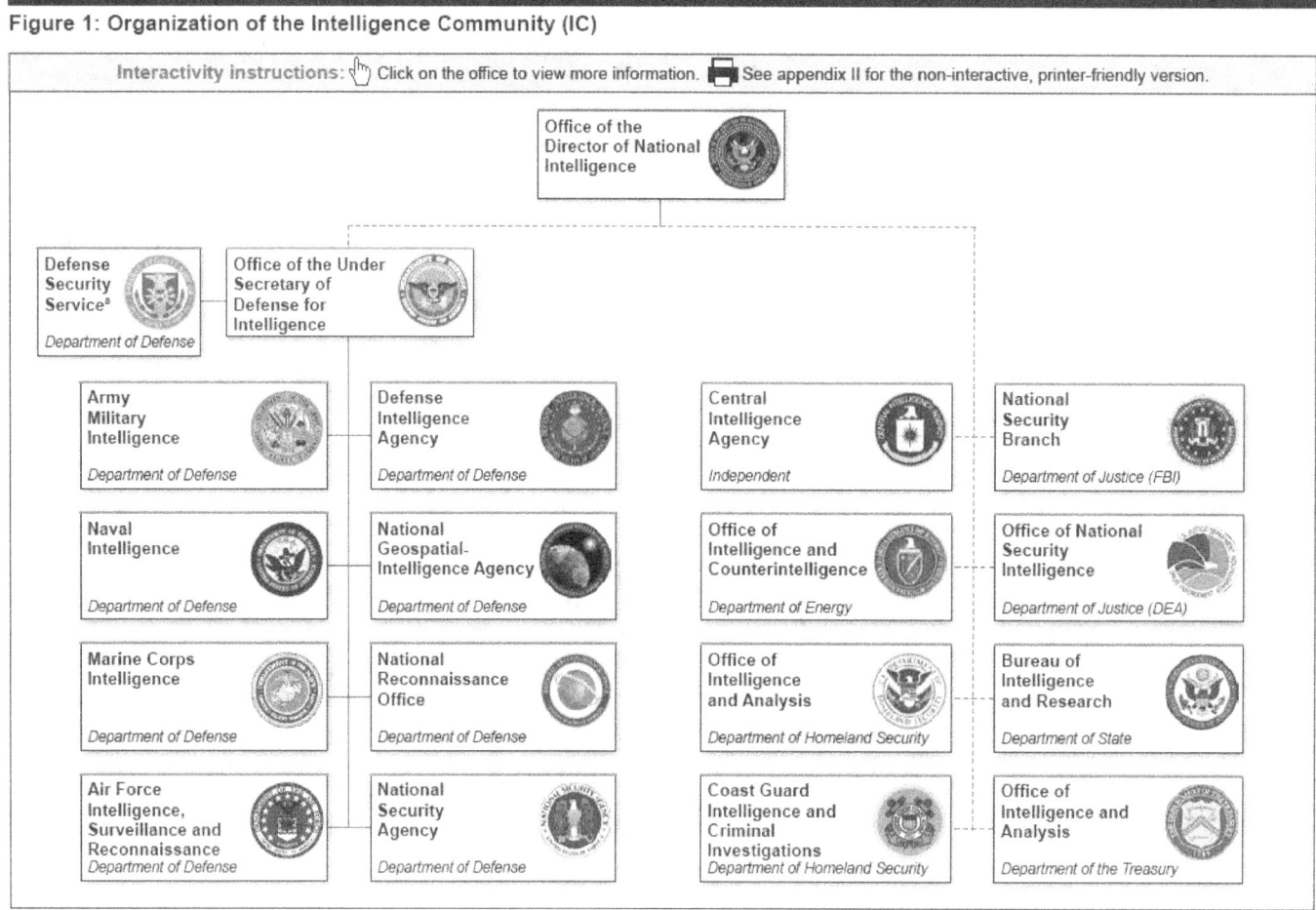

Interactivity instructions: 🖑 Click on the office to view more information. 🖨 See appendix II for the non-interactive, printer-friendly version.

Office of the Director of National Intelligence

Defense Security Service[a]
Department of Defense

Office of the Under Secretary of Defense for Intelligence

Army Military Intelligence
Department of Defense

Defense Intelligence Agency
Department of Defense

Central Intelligence Agency
Independent

National Security Branch
Department of Justice (FBI)

Naval Intelligence
Department of Defense

National Geospatial-Intelligence Agency
Department of Defense

Office of Intelligence and Counterintelligence
Department of Energy

Office of National Security Intelligence
Department of Justice (DEA)

Marine Corps Intelligence
Department of Defense

National Reconnaissance Office
Department of Defense

Office of Intelligence and Analysis
Department of Homeland Security

Bureau of Intelligence and Research
Department of State

Air Force Intelligence, Surveillance and Reconnaissance
Department of Defense

National Security Agency
Department of Defense

Coast Guard Intelligence and Criminal Investigations
Department of Homeland Security

Office of Intelligence and Analysis
Department of the Treasury

Source: GAO analysis of ODNI information.

[a] The DSS is not a component of the IC, but falls under the USDI and, under DOD policy, is a participant in the Joint Duty Program.

Establishment of the Joint Duty Program

IRTPA provides statutory authority to the Director of National Intelligence to create the Joint Duty Program. Specifically, IRTPA provides that ODNI shall prescribe mechanisms to facilitate the rotation of IC personnel through various elements of the IC in the course of their careers in order to facilitate the widest possible understanding by these personnel of the variety of intelligence requirements, methods, users, and capabilities. Such mechanisms may include establishing requirements for education, training, and evaluation for service involving more than one element of the IC.

Congress noted in IRTPA that the mechanisms prescribed for the Joint Duty Program should, to the extent practical, try to duplicate the joint officer management policies established by the Goldwater-Nichols Department of Defense Reorganization Act of 1986.[14] At the time Goldwater-Nichols was enacted, cultural change was needed to move DOD away from its service parochialisms toward interservice cooperation and coordination so that DOD could better prepare its military leaders to plan, support, and conduct joint, or multiservice, operations. Goldwater-Nichols required DOD to develop officers in joint matters through education, to assign officers who meet specified criteria to joint positions, and to factor this joint education and experience into its officer promotion decisions.

To help facilitate the transformation to a more integrated and collaborative Intelligence Community, in October 2007 ODNI released a 500 Day Plan that identified six key focus areas which contained core and enabling initiatives that ODNI planned to execute to deepen integration of the IC's people, processes, and technologies.[15] The first key focus area in the 500 Day Plan was creating a culture of collaboration, and a core initiative in the plan to address this area was implementing the civilian IC Joint Duty Program, which also included the design, development, and execution of the Joint Leadership Development Program. The Joint Leadership Development Program was intended to provide professional training and

---

[14]Pub. Law No. 99-433 (1986).

[15]United States Intelligence Community, *500 Day Plan: Integration and Collaboration* (Oct. 10, 2007). This document was a key source of strategic direction when the Joint Duty Program was initially implemented, and it emphasized the importance of training and education as part of the program. However, in June 2012 ODNI told us that this plan is now outdated and no longer provides strategic direction for ODNI.

education for employees who are participating in or who have completed a joint duty assignment.

Figure 2 provides a timeline of the key events surrounding the implementation of the Joint Duty Program.

Figure 2: Timeline of Key IC Joint Duty Related Events

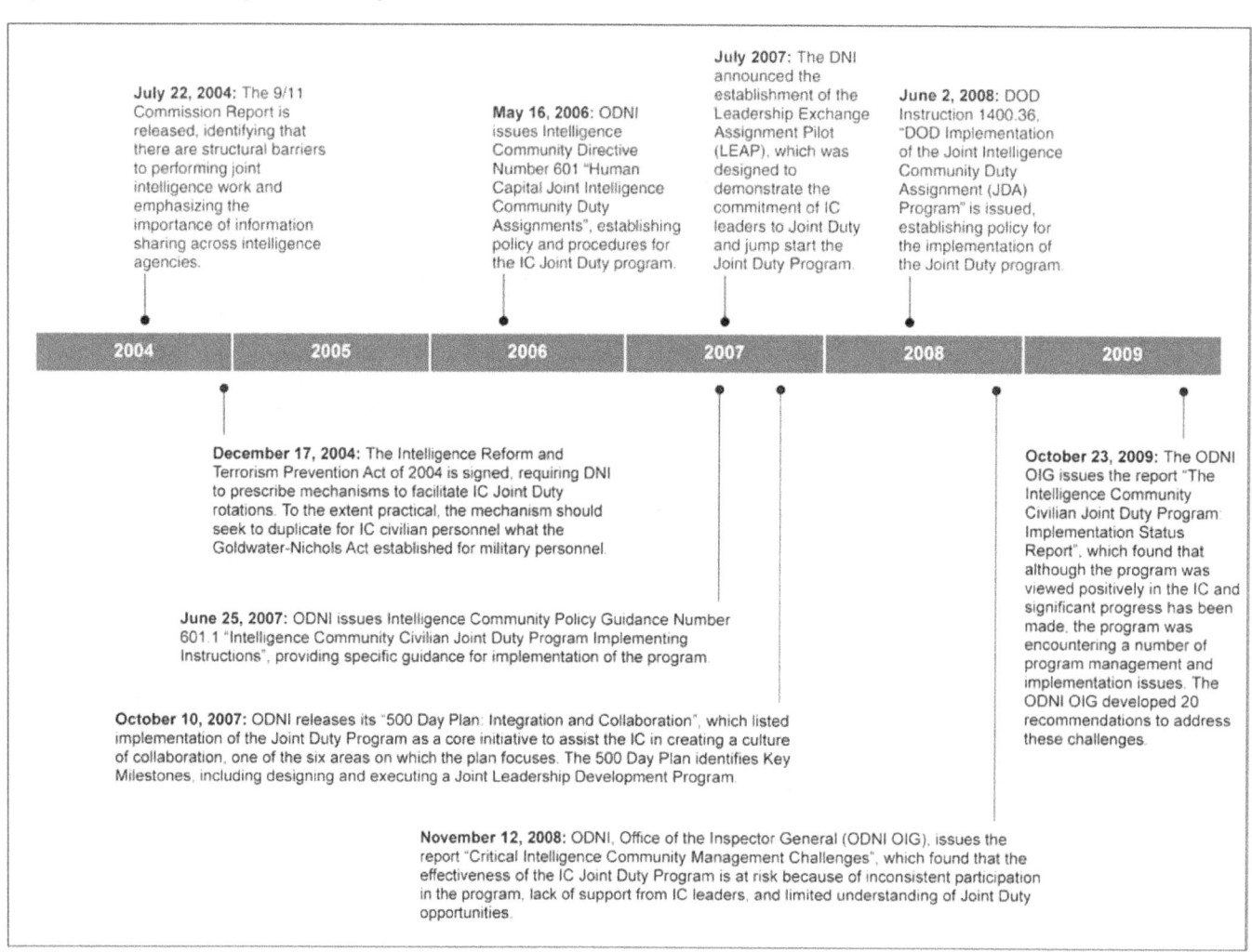

Source: GAO analysis

GAO-12-679 Intelligence Community Personnel

Process Employees Use to Apply for and Rotate to a Joint Duty Assignment

While individuals apply for joint duty assignments using the internal policies and procedures established by their home element, the basic procedures that employees must follow to apply for and rotate to a joint duty assignment are uniform, as established by ODNI guidance. Figure 3 provides an overview of these fundamental processes.

Figure 3: Process Employees Use to Apply for and Rotate to a Joint Duty Assignment

Employee decides to participate in joint duty program. Employee checks ODNI joint duty website for rotation vacancy announcements.	Employee's first- and second-level supervisors approve rotation. Employee applies and is selected for rotation vacancy.	Employee's home and gaining agency negotiate a memorandum of understanding to govern the rotation.	Employee completes rotation of at least 12 months while remaining permanent employee of home agency.	Employee is reintegrated back into home agency in former or an equivalent position.	Employee submits claim for and receives joint duty credit.

Source: GAO analysis of ODNI guidance

For a more complete overview of the Joint Duty Program, see appendix III.

All IC Elements Except for One Are Participating in the Joint Duty Program

To date, all of the IC elements are participating in the Joint Duty Program except for the U.S. Coast Guard,[16] and each of the participating IC elements has identified an agency-specific office or individual responsible for facilitating the Joint Duty Program at that level. Responsibilities of the office or individual responsible for facilitating the program include managing the rotations of personnel to other IC elements—for example, negotiating memorandums of understanding for assignments and adjudicating joint duty credit.[17] In addition, each IC element has some flexibility with respect to how its internal process for participating in the

---

[16] The U.S. Coast Guard is a component agency of the Department of Homeland Security.

[17] The ODNI has developed a standard memorandum of understanding that includes provisions governing rotational assignments and is used by all of the IC elements, who then tailor the provisions to govern each individual rotational assignment.

Joint Duty Program is implemented. As a result of this flexibility, several IC elements have established unique measures that facilitate the Joint Duty Program at their element. For example, the National Geospatial-Intelligence Agency preapproves individuals to participate in joint duty assignments prior to the application process to ensure that employees meet Joint Duty Program standard requirements, strategically places employees in appropriate rotational assignments, and plans for employees' return after their rotations. The U.S. Marine Corps has initiated a similar process. In addition, the Federal Bureau of Investigation is starting a mandatory "out-briefing" class for all personnel temporarily assigned to another organization, including Joint Duty Program participants. This class will cover issues that personnel commonly face while they are away from their home element, such as the way time and attendance should be handled and how the reintegration process will work. Furthermore, at the Department of State, returning joint duty participants complete presentations and brief co-workers through "Trade Craft" presentations, which serve as a forum to share knowledge gained during joint duty rotations.

IC officials cited enhanced collaboration, increased networking, and a better understanding of the community as a whole as positive aspects of the Joint Duty Program. Further, around half of the IC element officials we interviewed stated that senior-level agency leaders supported the program. Several officials noted that ODNI's monthly community of practice meetings for Joint Duty Program managers were a good way to share information about the program—for example, best practices regarding different IC elements' program implementation measures. Other IC element officials noted that the Joint Duty Program provides a benefit to their elements because personnel returning from joint duty assignments are able to leverage their new skills or knowledge to benefit the home element. Finally, officials from the IC elements identified one other benefit of the program—individuals rotating to other IC elements have a new opportunity to develop professionally.

The U.S. Coast Guard, however, has not participated in the Joint Duty Program. U.S. Coast Guard officials stated that its participation has been delayed because they plan to conduct a workforce study on developmental needs for their civilian personnel, which will include determining how the U.S. Coast Guard will participate in the Joint Duty Program. However, the U.S. Coast Guard has not identified a time frame for the completion of the workforce study and noted that the position assigned the responsibility for conducting the study is vacant because the U.S. Coast Guard is currently under a hiring freeze due to budgetary constraints. U.S. Coast Guard officials did note they have begun sending a representative to the ODNI Community of Practice meetings so that the U.S. Coast Guard can learn about joint duty best practices and challenges that other IC elements have faced. Nevertheless, IRTPA, Intelligence Community Directive 601, and DOD Instruction 1400.36[18] stipulate that the Joint Duty Program applies to the defined IC, which includes the U.S. Coast Guard's civilian intelligence personnel in its National Intelligence Element. Because the ODNI Joint Duty Program guidance states that joint duty credit is a mandatory qualification requirement in order for personnel to be eligible for promotion to any civilian position classified above the GS-15 level (such as Senior Executive Service positions), nonparticipation means that the U.S. Coast Guard may be unable to promote any of its civilian intelligence personnel to fill vacancies in intelligence positions at the senior executive level. Although Intelligence Community Policy Guidance 601.1 allows the requirement of joint duty certification for promotion to senior executive positions to be waived, ODNI officials stated they do not anticipate granting waivers in the future.[19] Although the U.S. Coast Guard's civilian intelligence workforce is smaller than those of most of the other IC elements, without the U.S. Coast Guard's participation in the Joint Duty Program, personnel in the other IC elements may not fully understand the U.S. Coast Guard's intelligence requirements, methods, users, and capabilities to secure the nation's ports and coastal waters. Further, the U.S. Coast Guard's IC employees may be missing an opportunity to better understand other IC elements' missions, cultures, and capabilities, apply that knowledge to achieving the U.S. Coast Guard's mission, and improve collaboration with other IC elements.

---

[18]Department of Defense Instruction 1400.36, *DOD Implementation of the Joint Intelligence Community Duty Assignment (JDA) Program* (June 2, 2008).

[19]The authority to grant joint duty waivers and exemptions may be exercised at the discretion of the Director of National Intelligence, and for Department of Defense IC agencies and elements, at the discretion of the Under Secretary of Defense for Intelligence, when designated as the Director of Defense Intelligence (DDI).

ODNI Has Not Established a Strategic Framework to Guide Implementation

ODNI Lacks a Strategic Framework

ODNI does not have a strategic framework to effectively guide the implementation of the Joint Duty Program. Our previous work has shown the importance of establishing a comprehensive and integrated strategic framework to help ensure successful organizational transformation.[20] Further, our prior work has demonstrated that having an effective plan for implementing programs and measuring progress can help decision makers determine whether initiatives are achieving desired results.[21] Specifically, we have reported that an effective plan for implementing a results-oriented strategic framework requires agencies to (1) clearly define a program's mission, (2) establish performance goals for which they will be held accountable and have quantifiable measures to gauge progress toward those goals, (3) determine strategies and resources to effectively accomplish those goals, (4) use performance information to make programmatic decisions necessary to make improvements, and (5) formally communicate results in performance reports.[22]

Accordingly, we reviewed and analyzed a variety of ODNI documents such as joint duty guidance, the Joint Duty Program's "IC Joint Duty Communications Strategy," and the Joint Duty Program's "Joint Duty

---

[20]GAO, *Defense Business Transformation: Achieving Success Requires a Chief Management Officer to Provide Focus and Sustained Leadership,* GAO-07-1072 (Washington, D.C.: Sept. 5, 2007).

[21]See for example, GAO, *Preventing Sexual Harassment: DOD Needs Greater Leadership Commitment and an Oversight Framework,* GAO-11-809 (Washington, D.C.: Sept. 21, 2011); *Government Performance: GPRA Modernization Act Provides Opportunities to Help Address Fiscal, Performance, and Management Challenges,* GAO-11-466T (Washington, D.C.: Mar. 16, 2011); *Military Personnel: DOD Needs an Oversight Framework and Standards to Improve Management of Its Casualty Assistance Programs,* GAO-06-1010 (Washington, D.C.: Sept. 22, 2006); *Results-Oriented Government: GPRA Has Established a Solid Foundation for Achieving Greater Results,* GAO-04-38 (Washington, D.C.: Mar. 10, 2004).

[22]GAO-11-809.

Vision, Mission, & Strategy" to determine if the components of a strategic framework existed either independently or as a single comprehensive framework. At the time of our review, ODNI's "Joint Duty Vision, Mission, & Strategy," for example, stated that the program's mission was to "create cross-agency expertise" and that the program's strategy was to "provide the workforce with opportunities for cross-agency collaboration and interdisciplinary experience." However, this document did not include the key components of a strategic framework, and neither does ODNI's joint duty directive or policy guidance. We found that although ODNI has taken some steps related to some of the components, such as collecting data on Joint Duty Program participation from the IC elements, opportunities for improvement exist in all components of a results-oriented strategic framework, as discussed below. Additionally, in May 2012, ODNI officials told us that their current "Joint Duty Vision, Mission, & Strategy" as well as its "IC Joint Duty Communications Strategy" were outdated, incomplete, and did not reflect the views of the current leadership.[23] ODNI officials also stated that these documents would be rewritten in their entirety; however, at the time of our review, officials indicated that no timeline for completion had been set.

Define the mission. Prior to ODNI's decision to rewrite its "Joint Duty Vision, Mission, & Strategy" noted above, some of the IC officials we interviewed stated that the Joint Duty Program mission is not clearly defined. As a result, IC elements interpret Joint Duty Program policy and guidance inconsistently. For some, the primary mission of joint duty assignments is to increase interagency collaboration, while for others, the mission is to enhance career development opportunities for individual participants. Additionally, ODNI guidance is unclear about whether joint duty assignments are intended for mission-critical employees or for those in support positions. In analyzing the IC elements' response to our data request for listings of the occupational series of program participants, we found that some elements afford opportunities for employees in support positions, such as human capital and administrative positions, to be regular participants in the program. At other elements, most program participants have mission-critical positions, such as intelligence analyst positions.

---

[23]The position of Assistant Director of National Intelligence for Human Capital and Intelligence Community Chief Human Capital Officer was last filled in November 2011. The position of Joint Duty Program Chief was last filled in March 2012.

In addition, although IRTPA requires the Director of National Intelligence to establish mechanisms to facilitate the rotation of IC personnel throughout the IC, ODNI guidance allows personnel participating in the Joint Duty Program to rotate outside of the IC or within their home element, which further exacerbates the lack of clarity in the program's mission. Of the 12 IC elements that responded to our data request with information about where their employees were completing the rotation, 10 IC elements reported that at least one person was currently rotating outside of the IC. We asked ODNI officials about these disparities and officials told us that the key expectations of a joint duty rotation are that the participant will complete work that is IC related, is at another element, and that the work can be justified as beneficial to the individual, the element, and the IC. The officials explained that a business case must be built for a person to receive joint duty credit outside of these key expectations.

Establish performance goals and measure progress toward those goals. Similarly, ODNI has not established specific performance goals or quantifiable metrics for measuring progress of the Joint Duty Program. We have previously reported that for planning and performance measurement to be effective, managers need to use performance information to identify performance problems and look for solutions, develop approaches that improve results, and make other important management decisions.[24] Intelligence Community Policy Guidance 601.1 established a requirement that all civilian IC personnel must have joint duty credit prior to being promoted to positions above the GS-15 level, a point that the Director of National Intelligence further articulated in a 2010 memorandum to the workforce. Since 2007, ODNI's Joint Duty Program Office has collected data about joint duty rotations from each IC element. While this information has been used to illustrate the promotion rates of joint duty participants and the number of personnel with joint duty credit, ODNI does not use these data in combination with defined goals to measure outcomes or program success. ODNI officials stated it aggregates the data collected and uses them to brief the Director of National Intelligence. Officials at several of the IC elements we met stated that the data fields identified and the frequency with which data are collected by the ODNI Joint Duty Program Office changed regularly with

---

[24]GAO, *Managing for Results: Enhancing Agency Use of Performance Information for Management Decision Making,* GAO-05-927 (Washington, D.C.: Sept. 9, 2005).

the turnover in the Joint Duty Program Office Chief position, making it difficult to identify trends and outcomes. Finally, officials at one element stated they have requested but not received feedback on the data they provide to ODNI. These officials noted, therefore, that they are unsure about whether they are providing the best possible data.

Identify resources. In addition, ODNI has not comprehensively identified resources needed to accomplish the mission of the Joint Duty Program. Financial resources dedicated to the Joint Duty Program vary significantly among the IC elements. For example, some IC elements have the financial resources to fill the positions left vacant when an employee leaves for a joint duty rotation and other IC elements struggle to absorb vacancies. An element's ability to plan financially is further complicated because joint duty positions vary with respect to whether they are "reimbursable" (the element receiving the new employee pays that employee's salary) or "non-reimbursable" (the element sending its employee to another element pays that employee's salary). In fact, one IC element stated it was instituting a formal policy that its employees cannot participate in joint duty rotations that are non-reimbursable, which may limit rotation opportunities for that element's employees. Other IC elements do not have a preference as to whether an employee accepts a reimbursable or non-reimbursable joint duty assignment.

ODNI has taken steps to address this issue by funding some positions left vacant during rotations. ODNI officials told us that these funds are disbursed on a first-come, first-served basis, and that IC elements making the request have to present a business case for their funding needs. To date, the officials said that the Drug Enforcement Administration, the U.S. Air Force, and the U.S. Navy have used the funds more often than other eligible IC elements. According to Intelligence Community Policy Guidance 601.1, six IC elements[25] cannot apply for these ODNI funds. At the time of our review, ODNI had identified resources to fund fewer than 50 non-reimbursable positions, but ODNI officials stated that they are able to meet the current demand with those funds.

Use performance information to make decisions for improvement. ODNI also has not consistently used performance information to make

---

[25]These six elements are the Central Intelligence Agency, the Defense Intelligence Agency, the Federal Bureau of Investigation, the National Geospatial-Intelligence Agency, the National Reconnaissance Office, and the National Security Agency.

decisions for improvement. While ODNI has used performance information and responded to recommendations from an ODNI Inspector General's 2009 report, this effort does not ensure an institutionalized method for monitoring improvement. In October 2009, the ODNI Office of the Inspector General issued a report reviewing the implementation of the Joint Duty Program,[26] which resulted in 20 recommendations that were intended to address the impediments affecting implementation of the program and to improve program participation. According to ODNI Inspector General officials, all of the recommendations have been closed and implemented. However, during the course of our review, we found that a number of challenges noted in the 2009 ODNI Inspector General report still existed. For example, the report found that the IC senior leaders and employees were confused about the purpose of the Joint Duty Program. In response to this finding, the report recommended that the ODNI Associate Director of National Intelligence/Chief Human Capital Office clarify the purpose of the Joint Duty Program to include both leadership development and broader collaboration throughout the IC. According to ODNI officials, the recommendation was closed and implemented. However, as we note in this report, the mission of the program remains unclear.

In addition to the 2009 Inspector General report, ODNI has developed an optional survey instrument for those individuals who have completed a joint duty rotation. However, because the survey is optional, at the time of our review ODNI had not collected enough responses for the results to be statistically significant. As a result, IC element officials we met stated they had not seen any of the results from these surveys and it is unclear how the results of these surveys are being used. Further, the ODNI Joint Duty Program Chief began a review of the Joint Duty Program in September 2011 with an estimated completion date of October 2011. ODNI officials stated that the preliminary results of the review were briefed to the Director of National Intelligence in December 2011. As of June 2012, this review was in draft and ODNI officials had not determined when a final report would be issued.

---

[26]Office of the Director of National Intelligence, Office of the Inspector General, *The Intelligence Community Civilian Joint Duty Program: Implementation Status Report,* CAS-2008-0003 (Washington, D.C.: October 2009). The investigation that led to this report was conducted at the request of the ODNI Chief Human Capital Officer, as a result of several impediments to the program that had been identified in a prior inspector general report on the status of integration and collaboration in the IC.

Communicate results. Finally, ODNI officials provided us with a document entitled "IC Joint Duty Communications Strategy", which is focused on increasing outreach and awareness of the program among the IC elements. While the ODNI officials stated, as noted above, that this document is being rewritten, we found that the document did not contain specific completion dates for the goals and activities identified. Moreover, it was not a plan for communicating results of a programmatic evaluation to the IC elements. The IC elements do not benefit from ODNI data calls or performance information collected from the voluntary surveys of joint duty participants because ODNI does not communicate their results to the IC elements. Although various demographic data are collected from each of the IC elements on a quarterly basis, this information is not made available or shared with the IC elements. ODNI officials we interviewed stated that they were unable to share results of the voluntary surveys with each of the IC elements because they did not have a representative sample of participants.

Joint Duty Program Has Experienced Repeated Leadership Turnover

Previous GAO reports have noted the significance of strong leadership support—both at the senior leadership and immediate supervisor level—as key to the successful implementation and oversight of programs, including interagency rotation programs.[27] Further, our work has shown that focused and sustained leadership is at the center of successful organizational transformation.[28] Our work has also shown that turnover in leadership can lead to critical gaps in institutional knowledge.[29]

---

[27]See for example, GAO, *Interagency Collaboration: State and Army Personnel Rotation Programs Can Build on Positive Results with Additional Preparation and Evaluation,* GAO-12-386 (Washington, D.C.: Mar. 9, 2012); *High-Risk Series: An Update,* GAO-11-278 (Washington, D.C.: February 2011); and *Defense Acquisitions: Strong Leadership Is Key to Planning and Executing Stable Weapons Programs,* GAO-10-522 (Washington, D.C.: May 6, 2010).

[28]See for example, GAO-07-1072 and GAO, *Defense Business Transformation: A Comprehensive Plan, Integrated Efforts, and Sustained Leadership Are Needed to Assure Success,* GAO-07-229T (Washington, D.C.: Nov. 16, 2006).

[29]See for example, GAO, *DHS Human Capital: Senior Leadership Vacancy Rate Generally Declined, but Components' Rates Varied,* GAO-12-264 (Washington, D.C.: Feb. 10, 2012); and *Older Workers: Federal Agencies Face Challenges but Have Opportunities to Hire and Retain Experienced Employees,* GAO-08-630T (Washington, D.C.: Apr. 30, 2008).

While the current Director of National Intelligence has emphasized the importance of the Joint Duty Program in creating a culture of collaboration in the IC, the Joint Duty Program Office Chief position—the individual responsible for implementing the program across the IC—has experienced repeated turnover since the program's inception. Specifically, since 2007, six different people have served in the Joint Duty Program Chief position, and five of these people have served in the Chief position over the last 3 years. Data provided by ODNI shows that terms of service for the last five incumbents in the Chief position have ranged from 4 months to 10 months. IC element officials noted that institutional knowledge within the ODNI Joint Duty Program office has not been transferred between Chiefs and that the different Chiefs have interpreted the program's mission and implementation differently, which in turn has led to confusion among the IC elements. For example, officials at one IC element stated that turnover of leadership at ODNI has made program implementation more difficult and has led to inconsistencies both in leadership styles and in program terminology.

Further, ODNI officials told us that, while all six Chiefs were senior executives, the Joint Duty Chief position had recently been downgraded from a Senior National Intelligence Service position to a General Schedule 15 position. The downgrade was made as part of a larger effort within ODNI to reduce the number of senior executive positions. Moreover, officials stated that in spring 2012, when the program Chief position was last filled, it was advertised as both a permanent and a joint duty assignment position.

Without an established comprehensive strategic framework that includes the key components to guide effective implementation, program efforts have been disjointed, and decision makers within ODNI have not had the information they need to successfully manage the Joint Duty Program. Such a strategic framework could transcend the turnovers in program leadership that the Joint Duty Program has repeatedly experienced.

ODNI Has Not Formally Established Professional Training and Education Programs to Support the Joint Duty Program

While ODNI has taken limited steps to establish the training and education component of the Joint Duty Program, to date ODNI has not formally established or implemented the training and education programs envisioned by IRTPA. IRTPA requires the Director of National Intelligence to prescribe, in consultation with the heads of the IC elements, personnel policies and programs that "set standards for education, training, and career development of personnel of the intelligence community." In 2007, the Director of National Intelligence issued Intelligence Community Policy Guidance 601.1, which indicates that the Director of National Intelligence intends to establish a Joint Leadership Development Program to provide professional training and education for employees who are participating in or who have completed a joint duty assignment. The guidance provides that completion of the Joint Leadership Development Program or an equivalent course of study will be required for personnel to be certified as having completed the Joint Duty Program, but waives this requirement until such time as the Director of National Intelligence establishes and implements the Joint Leadership Development Program. ODNI also identified the design, development, and execution of the Joint Leadership Development Program as part of a core initiative for its 500 day plan issued in 2007.[30] Approximately 5 years after ODNI's issuance of Intelligence Community Policy Guidance 601.1, however, ODNI has not formally established the Joint Leadership Development Program. In June 2012, ODNI told us that this program has been terminated.

Instead, ODNI has recently taken some steps to develop what ODNI officials call the "learning component" to the Joint Duty Program. In October 2011, ODNI officials identified the following three training courses that they had developed specifically for the Joint Duty Program to promote a culture of collaboration and integration across the IC: (1) Understanding the Intelligence Community, for employees new to the IC; (2) Integrating the Intelligence Community, for General Schedule-13 through General Schedule-15 IC personnel with management responsibilities; and (3) Leading the Intelligence Community, for Senior Executives. ODNI officials explained that Joint Duty Program participants would be expected to complete only one of the three courses. Further, on

---

[30]United States Intelligence Community, *500 Day Plan: Integration and Collaboration* (Oct. 10, 2007). This document was a key source of strategic direction for ODNI when the Joint Duty Program was initially implemented, and it emphasized the importance of training and education as part of the program. However, in June 2012 ODNI told us that this plan is now outdated and no longer provides strategic direction for ODNI.

GAO-12-679 Intelligence Community Personnel

October 4, 2011, the Director of National Intelligence issued a memo stating that the joint duty training requirement can be met by completing an existing degree or certificate program at the National Intelligence University.[31] ODNI officials also said that, in the future, ODNI may allow personnel to take other courses to receive joint duty training credit, but ODNI had not yet made a determination at the time of our audit work.

Currently, however, IC personnel are not required to take any of these three courses when participating in the Joint Duty Program because ODNI has not determined or documented in guidance what courses will make up the training component of the program. ODNI officials stated that they intend to revise Intelligence Community Directive 601 and Intelligence Community Policy Guidance 601.1 to provide a more detailed description of the training component than is provided currently in those documents. However, the officials did not have a time frame for when they expected the revisions to be completed and did not elaborate on how the guidance might be revised.

Accordingly, the extent to which Joint Duty Program participants who have completed joint duty rotations have taken any of the three courses developed for the Joint Duty Program is unclear. None of the IC elements whose officials responded to our request for attendance data indicated that any of their Joint Duty Program participants had received credit for taking any of the courses. Specifically, officials from nine IC elements reported that none of the personnel who have received joint duty credit had taken any of the courses, and officials from four IC elements reported that they did not track these data.

While ODNI noted that the three courses had received praise from some class participants in course evaluations that are administered at the conclusion of every course, during the course of our review officials from nine IC elements expressed concerns about the content and rigor of the three courses. Officials from three of the IC elements told us that the courses did not appear to be tailored to support the Joint Duty Program or correlate to the performance management standards for leadership. ODNI officials explained that because each of the IC elements has its own leadership development program, ODNI had opted for the courses to

---

[31]The National Intelligence University is a federal degree granting institution that educates and prepares intelligence officers to meet current and future challenges to the national security of the United States.

focus on developing a collaborative culture and an appreciation for other agencies' challenges. Officials from three other IC elements expressed concern that the courses could potentially duplicate or overlap with existing IC agency training courses. ODNI officials told us that they had not reviewed the IC elements' individual training courses since 2009. Finally, three other IC elements noted that the courses are not sufficiently rigorous, like academic year-long programs offered by U.S. military service war colleges or DOD's National Defense University. ODNI officials explained that they wanted to keep the classes short enough so that Joint Duty Program participants would not be taken offline for a long period of time to complete the training. The officials stated that unlike the military and its joint duty program, there is no capacity in the civilian IC workforce to replace personnel who are away at training.

Finally, at the time of our review, ODNI had not yet developed an implementation plan and timeline for the training component once the requirements are formally established. ODNI officials explained, for example, that they have not yet determined how to phase in the training across the IC, or whether personnel who have already completed joint duty rotations will be grandfathered, or exempted, from having to complete the training requirements. The officials stated that their key focus was on GS-15 personnel, as that was the population where personnel must have the joint duty credit in order to be promoted. The officials added that when ODNI moves forward with implementation of the training component of the Joint Duty Program, they will either grandfather personnel or set a date by which participants must have completed the required training. Until the training and education component of the Joint Duty Program is fully developed and a timeline established for implementation, the program may be unable to fully succeed in its goal of achieving the widest possible understanding of IC personnel of various intelligence requirements, methods, users, and capabilities, which could hinder IC efforts to work together and collaborate to prevent or counter terrorism.

Conclusions

IRTPA empowers the Director of National Intelligence to create a Joint Duty Program that could more fully integrate the IC by helping to remove or reduce the significant institutional, cultural, and organizational factors that impeded the IC from operating in an effective and collaborative manner. To date, however, the Joint Duty Program remains a disjointed effort. The IC elements—with the exception of the U.S. Coast Guard, which plans on first conducting a workforce study on developmental needs for their civilian personnel to help determine how they will participate in the Joint Duty Program—have responded by taking element-specific steps to actively participate in the Joint Duty Program. Nonetheless, repeated turnover in the Joint Duty Program Office's Chief position (five Chiefs in the past 3 years), has hindered development of a strategic plan that could enhance the clarity of the Joint Duty Program's mission, measure progress towards goals, and instill accountability in achieving those goals. The fact that ODNI has identified a need to modify or rewrite the Joint Duty Program's directive, policy guidance, "Joint Duty Vision, Mission, & Strategy" and "IC Joint Duty Communications Strategy", further highlights the need to develop a strategic framework to provide a clear road map to guide the Joint Duty Program. The absence of a strategic framework coupled with turnover of personnel in the Chief position has limited ODNI's ability to foster the institutional knowledge that transcends turnovers in program leadership and is necessary to sustain the Joint Duty Program and more fully integrate the IC through joint assignments. The same is true for the training component of the Joint Duty Program. The fact that the training component remains unfocused and unimplemented means the program is missing an essential element to provide for cross-agency understanding and collaboration. Absent the development of a comprehensive strategic framework to guide program implementation and of formal training requirements with a plan to implement them, the Joint Duty Program is not positioned to foster the widest possible understanding of intelligence requirements, methods, users, and capabilities.

Recommendations for Executive Action

To help ensure that personnel in all of the IC elements fully understand the U.S. Coast Guard's intelligence mission to secure the nation's ports and coastal waters, that the U.S. Coast Guard's civilian intelligence employees do not miss an opportunity to develop collaborative relationships with and to understand other IC elements, and that U.S. Coast Guard civilians remain viable for promotion to senior positions requiring joint duty credit, we recommend that the Secretary of Homeland Security direct the Commandant of the U.S. Coast Guard to take steps to participate in the Joint Duty Program consistent with ODNI policy and guidance.

To improve the effectiveness of the implementation of the Joint Duty Program and to help ensure that institutional knowledge about the program transcends the individual tenure of each serving Joint Duty Program Chief, we recommend that the Director of National Intelligence develop a comprehensive strategic framework for the Joint Duty Program. This framework could include things such as

- clearly defining its mission,
- establishing performance goals,
- developing quantifiable metrics for measuring progress toward achieving performance goals,
- determining the financial resources necessary to accomplish the mission of the program,
- using performance information and metrics to make decisions to improve the program, and
- communicating results effectively with each of the IC elements.

To implement those provisions of IRTPA that address joint training and education and facilitate the widest possible understanding and collaboration among the IC, we recommend that the Director of National Intelligence take the following two actions:

- Establish formal training and education requirements for the Joint Duty Program, revise the existing policy guidance to clearly identify and describe these requirements, and eliminate the waiver that is currently in the guidance; and
- Develop a formal plan and timeline to implement the training and education component of the Joint Duty Program.

Agency Comments and Our Evaluation

We provided a draft of this report to the Department of Homeland Security and ODNI for review and comment. In written comments, the Department of Homeland Security agreed with the recommendation regarding the U.S. Coast Guard, and cited actions being taken to implement a joint duty program at the U.S. Coast Guard. The Department of Homeland Security's comments are reprinted in their entirety in appendix IV. ODNI generally agreed with our three recommendations addressed to it, and provided two specific comments related to our findings. ODNI's comments are reprinted in their entirety in appendix V. ODNI also provided a number of general and technical comments that we considered and incorporated, as appropriate.

The Department of Homeland Security noted that they and the U.S. Coast Guard agreed with our first recommendation that the U.S. Coast Guard take steps to participate in the Joint Duty Program consistent with ODNI policy and guidance. The Department of Homeland Security stated that establishing a formal civilian Joint Duty Program was one of the U.S. Coast Guard's many human resource priorities, and that policy and guidance was presently being developed for such a program. The Department of Homeland Security also stated that it believes the U.S. Coast Guard is operating within the spirit of the Joint Duty Program with regard to information sharing, collaboration, and professional development due to its military intelligence positions that are assigned to other agencies. They noted that the U.S. Coast Guard anticipates making significant progress in developing its civilian Joint Duty Program in the coming months, and noted specific actions that will be taken to do this. ODNI did not comment on this recommendation and, instead, deferred to the U.S. Coast Guard for a formal response.

ODNI agreed with our second recommendation to develop a comprehensive strategic framework for the Joint Duty Program, which could include things such as clearly defining its mission, establishing performance goals, developing quantifiable metrics for measuring progress toward achieving performance goals, determining the financial resources necessary to accomplish the mission of the program, using performance information and metrics to make decisions to improve the program, and communicating results effectively with each of the IC elements. ODNI stated that the Joint Duty Program would benefit from a single comprehensive strategic document, and noted that the Director of National Intelligence has requested that a program strategy be developed to help guide the program. ODNI expressed appreciation for GAO's guidance. As we note in our report, a comprehensive and integrated strategic framework can help ensure successful organizational transformation and can help effectively guide implementation.

ODNI partially agreed with our third recommendation that ODNI establish formal training and education requirements for the Joint Duty Program, revise the existing policy guidance to clearly identify and describe these requirements, and eliminate the waiver that is presently in the guidance. ODNI also partially agreed with our fourth recommendation that ODNI develop a formal plan and timeline to implement the training and education component of the joint duty program. While ODNI's comments treated these two recommendations as one recommendation in its response, we consider these to be two separate recommendations that will require separate, independent actions from ODNI to implement. In its response, ODNI explained that it agreed that ODNI needed to provide formal guidance regarding the learning component to the Joint Duty Program, and stated that it would develop this guidance in conjunction with its revision of the Joint Duty Program policy. However, in responding to these recommendations, ODNI also stated that it did not concur with GAO's assertion that the current program is not fully complying with the requirements of the IRTPA, noting that section 102A(I)(3)(B) of IRTPA states only that the program "*may* include . . . the establishment of requirements for education, training, service, and evaluation for service

involving more than one element of the intelligence community"
[emphasis added by ODNI]. Our recommendations are based on an
assessment of the steps ODNI has taken to implement the training,
education, and joint duty elements contained in IRTPA, and are intended
to enhance that implementation. We modified the language in the
recommendation to address ODNI's concerns regarding compliance with
IRTPA. We continue to believe that ODNI should revise its existing policy
guidance to formally establish and clearly identify and describe the
training component of the Joint Duty Program. Further, as we discussed
in our report, ODNI first formalized its intention to establish a training
program as part of the Joint Duty Program in its policy guidance 5 years
ago, but ODNI has not made substantive progress in implementing this
program. Therefore, we continue to believe that the ODNI should develop
a formal plan and timeline to implement the training and education
component of the Joint Duty Program.

In addition to generally agreeing with our three recommendations directed
to the Director of National Intelligence, ODNI provided two specific
comments related to our findings:

* Related to our statement in the report that ODNI has not established
  specific performance goals or quantifiable metrics for measuring
  progress of the Joint Duty Program, ODNI asserted that that the
  statement is inaccurate. ODNI noted that the Joint Duty Program's
  key performance goal is that all IC officers earn joint duty credit prior
  to promotion above the GS-15 level. ODNI also stated that as of its
  last data call in the fall of 2011, all but one person had been promoted
  with joint duty credit. ODNI further stated that it collects additional
  data on the total number of civilian personnel in the IC with joint duty
  credit. While we agree that ODNI collects this information, we believe
  that these data do not go far enough to effectively measure the
  success of the Joint Duty Program. As we note in our report, for
  performance measures to be effective, information should be used to
  identify performance problems and corresponding solutions, develop
  approaches that improve results, and make other important
  management decisions. The data ODNI collects, however, do not
  provide information about whether joint duty participants are obtaining
  the widest possible understanding of the IC. We note in the report that
  IRTPA requires the Director of National Intelligence to facilitate the
  rotation of IC personnel to other IC elements in order to obtain the
  widest possible understanding of the range of intelligence
  requirements, methods, users, and capabilities. Furthermore, the
  promotion rate data that ODNI collects does not differentiate between

those personnel in the IC who earned joint duty credit through the Joint Duty Program and those personnel in the IC who were granted joint duty credit for experiences that predate the creation of the Joint Duty Program in 2006. According to ODNI policy guidance, joint duty credit is granted for joint duty experience completed as far back as September 11, 2001. We also note in our report that ODNI currently administers surveys to IC personnel upon completion of their joint duty assignment. These surveys could potentially provide a mechanism to measure the quality of the Joint Duty Program and determine if IC personnel are gaining an understanding of the range of intelligence requirements, methods, and capabilities of the IC. However, as we note in the report, these surveys are optional. In addition, ODNI has not collected a sufficient number of these surveys to make the results meaningful, and it has not shared the information collected with the IC components. We have previously reported that successful performance measurement provides useful information for decisionmaking.[32] Further, the Standards for Internal Control in the Federal Government note that management should track major achievements and compare actual performance to planned or expected results to analyze significant differences. [33]

- ODNI also disagreed with our statement that without an established comprehensive strategic framework that includes the key components to guide effective implementation, and that transcends program leader turnover, program efforts have been disjointed, and decisionmakers within ODNI have not had the information they need to successfully manage the Joint Duty Program. In its written comments, ODNI stated that the Joint Duty Program is a key tool to integrating the IC. ODNI further stated that the program has met the performance measures identified in Intelligence Community Directive 601. Finally, ODNI stated that, while it agrees that a comprehensive strategic plan could be beneficial to the Joint Duty Program, it disagrees that the program has been unsuccessful without such a document. We agree that the Joint Duty Program can be a key tool in integrating the IC. In our report, we note that IC officials we met stated that enhanced collaboration, increased networking, and a better understanding of the

---

[32]GAO, *Tax Administration: IRS Needs to Further Refine Its Tax Filing Season Performance Measures,* GAO-03-143 (Washington, D.C.: Nov. 22, 2002).

[33]GAO, *Standards for Internal Control in the Federal Government,* GAO-AIMD-00-21.3.1 (Washington, D.C.: November 1999).

community as a whole were positive aspects of the Joint Duty Program. We disagree, however, with ODNI's statement that Intelligence Community Directive 601 contains performance measures. We noted above that ODNI collects data on joint duty participants, but collection of these data elements is not included or outlined in the directive. We continue to believe that a results-oriented strategic framework is important for implementing programs because it helps agencies to define a program's mission, establish performance goals and measures, identify needed resources, use performance information to inform decisions, and communicate results.

As we state in the report, ODNI has taken steps related to some of the components of a strategic framework, such as by providing some funding for positions left vacant during rotations, responding to recommendations from the ODNI Inspector General's 2009 report, and collecting data on Joint Duty Program participation. However, opportunities exist for improvement in all areas. For example, we reported that ODNI does not consistently use the data it collects to measure program success and does not communicate survey results or data collection results with the IC elements. It is even more critical for a comprehensive strategic framework to be in place in the absence of stability in key leadership positions such as the Joint Duty Program Chief. As we reported, the Joint Duty Program Chief has experienced repeated turnover (five Chiefs in the past 3 years), with tenure lasting between 4 months to 10 months, and IC element officials we met with expressed concern that institutional knowledge is not transferred between Chiefs. During the course of our own audit work, in fact, there was a 3 month gap between tenures of Joint Duty Program Chiefs. As such, we believe that our statement that the Joint Duty Program efforts have been disjointed is merited. We state in our report that sustained leadership is at the center of successful organizational transformation and that turnover in leadership can lead to critical gaps in institutional knowledge. In its comments, ODNI concurred with our recommendation to develop a strategic plan that transcends turnover at the Joint Duty Program Chief Position, which can help ensure successful organizational transformation and can help effectively guide implementation.

We are sending copies of this report to interested congressional committees, the Director of National Intelligence, the Commandant of the U.S. Coast Guard, the U.S. Attorney General, the Director of the Central Intelligence Agency, and the Secretaries of Defense, Energy, Homeland Security, State, and Treasury. In addition, the report is available at no charge on the GAO website at http://www.gao.gov.

If you or your staff have any questions about this report, please contact me at (202) 512-3604 or farrellb@gao.gov. Contact points for our Offices of Congressional Relations and Public Affairs may be found on the last page of this report. GAO staff who made key contributions to this report are listed in appendix VI.

Brenda S. Farrell
Director, Defense Capabilities
   and Management

Appendix I: Scope and Methodology

The scope of our review of the Intelligence Community (IC) Civilian Joint Duty Program (Joint Duty Program) included the Office of the Director of National Intelligence (ODNI), which is responsible for establishing policy and procedures for the Joint Duty Program across the IC; the 16 remaining IC components;[1] the Office of the Under Secretary of Defense for Intelligence in its capacity as the oversight entity for the Department of Defense (DOD) IC elements; and the Defense Security Service, because its civilian personnel fall under the Office of the Under Secretary of Defense for Intelligence and are subject, under DOD policy, to the IC Joint Duty Program requirements.

We obtained relevant documentation and interviewed key officials from the following offices within each IC element:

- Office of the Director of National Intelligence
  - Human Capital Office,
- Office of the Under Secretary of Defense for Intelligence
  - Defense Intelligence Agency
    - Directorate for Human Capital
  - National Geospatial-Intelligence Agency
    - Career Development Division
  - National Security Agency
    - Joint Duty Program Office
  - National Reconnaissance Office
    - Office of Strategic Human Capital

---

[1]The U.S. Intelligence Community comprises 17 components. The Office of the Director of National Intelligence oversees the Intelligence Community, and is counted as one of the 17 components. The other 16 components are: the National Security Agency, National Geospatial-Intelligence Agency, National Reconnaissance Office, Defense Intelligence Agency, Army Intelligence, Navy Intelligence, Marine Corps Intelligence, Air Force Intelligence (Air Force Intelligence, Surveillance, and Reconnaissance), Central Intelligence Agency, Department of Homeland Security (Office of Intelligence and Analysis), Department of State (Bureau of Intelligence and Research), Department of Treasury (Office of Intelligence and Analysis), Federal Bureau of Investigation (National Security Branch), Drug Enforcement Administration (Office of National Security Intelligence), U.S. Coast Guard (Intelligence and Criminal Investigations), and Department of Energy (Office of Intelligence and Counterintelligence).

- The intelligence elements within the military services
  - U.S. Army
    - Intelligence Personnel Management and Operations
  - U.S. Navy
    - Naval Intelligence, Human Capital Office
  - U.S. Marine Corps
    - Intelligence Department, Human Capital Office
  - U.S. Air Force
    - Intelligence, Surveillance, and Reconnaissance Force Development
  - Defense Security Service
    - Office of Human Resources,
- Central Intelligence Agency
  - Corporate Human Resources Programs,
- Department of Energy
  - Office of Intelligence and Counterintelligence,
- Department of Homeland Security
  - Office of Intelligence and Analysis
  - Office of Human Capital
  - U.S. Coast Guard
    - Office of Intelligence Workforce Management,
- Department of Justice
  - Federal Bureau of Investigation
    - Law Enforcement and Intelligence Community Liaison Office
  - Drug Enforcement Administration
    - Office of National Security Intelligence,
- Department of State
  - Bureau of Intelligence and Research, and
- Department of the Treasury
  - Office of Intelligence and Analysis.

Additionally, we interviewed officials from the National Intelligence University to ascertain the extent to which they support the Joint Duty Program.

To evaluate the extent to which IC elements are participating in the Joint Duty Program, we interviewed cognizant agency officials and reviewed available program documentation and guidance from ODNI, the Office of the Under Secretary of Defense for Intelligence, and the Joint Duty Program offices (or similar entity) of each of the IC elements.

To evaluate the extent to which ODNI has developed a strategic framework to help ensure the effective implementation of the Joint Duty Program across the IC, we reviewed the sections of the Intelligence Reform and Terrorism Prevention Act of 2004[2] (IRTPA) related to the establishment of the Joint Duty Program. We also reviewed governmentwide accepted best practices for program implementation along with previous GAO reports,[3] and compared these with the implementation of the Joint Duty Program. We also obtained and reviewed the ODNI Inspector General's report on the Joint Duty Program[4] to further identify and describe challenges that existed in implementing the Joint Duty Program as well as to ascertain if any lessons learned were identified. In addition, we conducted structured interviews with cognizant agency officials within each of the IC elements to determine the approach each IC element is taking in implementing the Joint Duty Program and to help identify challenges to the program's implementation as well as any lessons learned that can be derived from the IC elements' perspectives. Finally, we requested data for fiscal years 2010 and 2011 on program participants from ODNI, the Office of the Under Secretary of

---

[2]Pub. L. No. 108-458, § 1011 (2004) (amending § 102A of the National Security Act of 1947, as codified at 50 U.S.C. § 403-1).

[3]GAO, *Preventing Sexual Harassment: DOD Needs Greater Leadership Commitment and an Oversight Framework,* GAO-11-809 (Washington, D.C.: Sept. 21, 2011); *Government Performance: GPRA Modernization Act Provides Opportunities to Help Address Fiscal, Performance, and Management Challenges,* GAO-11-466T (Washington, D.C.: Mar. 16, 2011); *Military Personnel: DOD Needs an Oversight Framework and Standards to Improve Management of Its Casualty Assistance Programs,* GAO-06-1010 (Washington, D.C.: Sept. 22, 2006); *Results-Oriented Government: GPRA Has Established a Solid Foundation for Achieving Greater Results,* GAO-04-38 (Washington, D.C.: Mar. 10, 2004).

[4]Office of the Director of National Intelligence, Office of the Inspector General, *The Intelligence Community Civilian Joint Duty Program: Implementation Status Report,* CAS-2008-0003 (Washington, D.C.: October 2009).

Defense for Intelligence, the Defense Security Service, and the IC components—including participant-specific data on: where joint duty rotations took place, rotation start and end dates, pay-grade and job series of the participant, how joint duty credit was earned (i.e., joint assignment, combat deployment, task force), whether or not the participant was granted a waiver, and whether or not the participant had completed a Joint Duty Certified Intelligence Learning Network Course.[5] In response to our data request, 12 IC elements provided data on an individual level, as we specifically requested.[6] Further, to assess the reliability of the data, we discussed these data with knowledgeable officials at the respective IC element to gain an understanding of the processes and databases used to collect and record data and to understand existing data quality control procedures and known limitations of the data. We found the data were sufficiently reliable to ascertain the characteristics of IC personnel participating in the Joint Duty Program in fiscal years 2010 and 2011.

To evaluate the extent to which ODNI has established training and education programs to support the Joint Duty Program, we reviewed legislative language in IRTPA that establishes expectations for joint training and education and compared actions ODNI is taking against the legislative criteria. To determine the actions ODNI had taken to establish training requirements, we reviewed ODNI guidance, including Intelligence Community Directive 601[7] and Intelligence Community Policy Guidance 601.1,[8] descriptions of three training courses that ODNI officials explained

---

[5]We did not collect personally identifying information for any joint duty participants.

[6]Army Intelligence, Navy Intelligence, Marine Corps Intelligence, Air Force Intelligence, National Geospatial-Intelligence Agency, Department of Energy, Department of the Treasury, Department of Homeland Security Office of Intelligence and Analysis, Defense Security Service, Drug Enforcement Administration, the Office of the Under Secretary of Defense for Intelligence, and Defense Intelligence Agency provided data on an individual level and were included in our analysis. The Central Intelligence Agency, Department of State, Director of National Intelligence, National Security Agency, and Federal Bureau of Investigation provided data on an aggregate level and data were not included in our analysis. The U.S. Coast Guard did not provide data because, as we note in this report, it did not have a Joint Duty Program at the time of our review. Similarly, the National Reconnaissance Office did not provide data because employees on a joint duty rotation are accounted for by their home agency.

[7]Intelligence Community Directive 601, *Human Capital: Joint Intelligence Community Duty Assignments* (May 16, 2006) (as amended Sept. 4, 2009).

[8]Intelligence Community Policy Guidance 601.1, *Intelligence Community Civilian Joint Duty Program Implementing Instructions* (June 25, 2007) (as amended Sept. 4, 2009).

would be used to meet the training and education requirement in the future, and other documents, such as the ODNI 500 day plan[9] and the 2009 ODNI Inspector General Report. In addition, we spoke with officials from ODNI and the National Intelligence University regarding efforts that had been undertaken to develop and implement the training and education component of the Joint Duty Program, and any challenges associated with implementation. We also met with officials from all of the IC elements to gain their perspectives on the actions ODNI had taken to establish training and education requirements for the Joint Duty Program. Furthermore, we requested and analyzed data from all of the IC elements to determine the extent that program participants had already completed any of the training courses that potentially would be required as part of the Joint Duty Program.

We conducted this performance audit from January 2010[10] through June 2012 in accordance with generally accepted government auditing standards. Those standards require that we plan and perform the audit to obtain sufficient, appropriate evidence to provide a reasonable basis for our findings and conclusions based on our audit objectives. We believe that the evidence obtained provides a reasonable basis for our findings and conclusions based on our audit objectives.

---

[9]United States Intelligence Community, *500 Day Plan: Integration and Collaboration* (Oct. 10, 2007).

[10]We initially began this engagement in January 2010, and notified the ODNI of our intention to schedule an entrance conference in early February. At the end of March 2010, ODNI provided us with a copy of the ODNI Office of the Inspector General, *The Intelligence Community Civilian Joint Duty Program: Implementation Status Report*, CAS-2008-0003 (Washington, D.C.: October 2009). We initially agreed with ODNI to postpone the entrance conference pending our review of their report. Subsequently, section 348 of the Intelligence Authorization Act for Fiscal Year 2010, Pub. L. No. 111-259 (2010), directed ODNI, in consultation with the Comptroller General, to develop a written directive governing GAO's access to information from elements of the IC. Pending issuance of this guidance, we suspended this engagement temporarily. The ODNI issued guidance in April 2011, accompanied by comments from the Comptroller General, and work on this engagement resumed in August 2011. See *Intelligence Community Directive 114: Comptroller General Access to Intelligence Community Information* (effective June 30, 2011).

Appendix II: Noninteractive Graphic and Text for Figure 1

Organization of the Intelligence Community (IC)

Element	Duties
Office of the Director of National Intelligence (ODNI)	The Intelligence Reform and Terrorism Prevention Act (IRTPA) of 2004 established the position of Director of National Intelligence with the responsibilities of serving as head of the IC, acting as the principal adviser to the President and National Security Council on intelligence matters, and overseeing and directing the implementation of the National Intelligence Program.
Office of the Under Secretary of Defense for Intelligence (OUSDI) Department of Defense	OUSDI is the principal staff element of the Secretary of Defense for matters relating to intelligence. The Under Secretary also serves as the Director of Defense Intelligence, acting as the primary military intelligence advisor to the Office of the Director of National Intelligence.
Defense Intelligence Agency (DIA) Department of Defense	DIA is a major producer and manager of foreign military intelligence for the Department of Defense. DIA provides timely, objective, all-source military intelligence to policy makers, to U.S. armed forces around the world, and to the DOD acquisition community and force planners to counter a variety of threats and challenges across the spectrum of conflict.
National Geospatial-Intelligence Agency (NGA) Department of Defense	NGA is a Department of Defense combat support agency and a member of the IC. NGA develops imagery and map-based intelligence solutions for U.S. national defense, homeland security, and safety of navigation.
National Reconnaissance Office (NRO) Department of Defense	NRO is a joint organization under the Department of Defense engaged in research and development, acquisition, launch, and operation of overhead reconnaissance systems necessary to meet the needs of the IC and the Department of Defense. The NRO workforce includes personnel assigned to the NRO primarily from the Air Force, the CIA, and the Navy. However, the other uniformed services and other elements of the Department of Defense and the IC are also represented.
National Security Agency (NSA) Department of Defense	NSA is the United States' cryptologic organization, with responsibility for protecting U.S. national security information systems and collecting and disseminating foreign signals intelligence. Areas of expertise include cryptanalysis, cryptography, mathematics, computer science, and foreign language analysis. NSA is part of the Department of Defense, and is staffed by a combination of civilian and military personnel.
Army Military Intelligence Department of the Army	Army Military Intelligence formulates Army intelligence policy, plans, programs, and budgets and oversees Army-level multidiscipline intelligence operations, intelligence support to Computer Network Operations, military intelligence personnel, training, readiness and equipping, security, foreign liaison and future threats.
Naval Intelligence Department of the Navy	The Office of Naval Intelligence is a major IC production center for maritime intelligence, analyzing and producing assessments of foreign naval capabilities, trends, operations and tactics, global civil maritime activity, and an extensive array of all-source analytical products.
Marine Corps Intelligence Department of the Navy	Marine Corps Intelligence produces tactical and operational intelligence for tactical and operational commanders and their staffs, as well as for other customers. Its IC component is comprised of all intelligence professionals in the Marine Corps. Most Marine Corps intelligence professionals are integrated into operating forces at all echelons of command from battalion/squadron to Marine Expeditionary Force.
Air Force Intelligence, Surveillance and Reconnaissance (ISR) Department of the Air Force	The Air Force Intelligence Surveillance and Reconnaissance Agency organizes, trains, equips, and presents assigned forces and capabilities to conduct ISR for Combatant Commanders and the nation. It implements and oversees the execution of Air Force headquarters policy and guidance to expand Air Force ISR capabilities to meet current and future challenges.

Defense Security Service Department of Defense	Defense Security Service is a Department of Defense support agency that supports national security and the warfighter. Defense Security Service clears industrial facilities, personnel, and associated information systems. Defense Security Service also secures the nation's technological base and oversees the protection of classified information. Although the Defense Security Service is not part of the IC, Defense Security Service falls under the USDI and is subject to the Joint Duty Program requirement as a matter of DOD policy.
Central Intelligence Agency (CIA)	CIA is the largest producer of all-source national security intelligence to senior U.S. policy makers. The CIA's intelligence analysis on overseas developments informs decisions by policy makers and other senior decision makers in the national security and defense arenas.
Office of Intelligence and Counterintelligence Department of Energy	Department of Energy's Office of Intelligence and Counterintelligence is the IC's premier technical intelligence resource in four core areas: nuclear weapons and nonproliferation; energy security; science and technology; and nuclear energy, safety, and waste.
Coast Guard Intelligence and Criminal Investigations Department of Homeland Security	Coast Guard Intelligence and Criminal Investigations directs, coordinates, and oversees intelligence and investigative operations and activities that support all Coast Guard objectives by providing actionable intelligence to strategic decision makers, as well as operational and tactical commanders.
Office of Intelligence and Analysis Department of Homeland Security (DHS)	DHS's Office of Intelligence and Analysis is DHS's headquarters intelligence element. It uses information and intelligence from multiple sources to identify and assess current and future threats to the United States. The Office of Intelligence and Analysis focuses on threats related to border security; chemical, biological, radiological, and nuclear issues, to include explosives and infectious diseases; critical infrastructure protection; extremists within the homeland; and travelers entering the homeland.
Office of National Security Intelligence Department of Justice (Drug Enforcement Administration)	The Drug Enforcement Administration's Office of National Security Intelligence leverages the global law enforcement drug intelligence assets of the Drug Enforcement Administration to report on matters relating to national security. Its goal is to enhance U.S. efforts to protect national security and combat global terrorism, as well as facilitate IC support to the Drug Enforcement Administration's law enforcement mission. Office of National Security Intelligence facilitates intelligence coordination and information sharing with other members of the IC and homeland security elements.
National Security Branch Department of Justice (Federal Bureau of Investigation)	The National Security Branch of the Federal Bureau of Investigation is a threat-based, intelligence driven, national security organization that protects the United States from critical threats while safeguarding civil liberties. As both a component of the Department of Justice and a full member of the U.S. IC, the Federal Bureau of Investigation serves as a vital link between intelligence and law enforcement agencies.
Bureau of Intelligence and Research Department of State	State's Bureau of Intelligence and Research (INR) serves as the focal point within the Department of State for all policy issues and activities involving the IC. INR analysts draw on all-source intelligence, diplomatic reporting, INR's public opinion polling, and interaction with U.S. and foreign scholars, covering all countries and regional or transnational issues.
Office of Intelligence and Analysis Department of the Treasury	Treasury's Office of Intelligence and Analysis receives, analyzes, collates, and disseminates foreign intelligence and foreign counterintelligence information related to the operation and responsibilities of the Department of the Treasury. OIA's strategic priorities are terrorist financing, insurgency financing, and rogue regimes/proliferation financing.

Source: GAO analysis of ODNI information.

Appendix III: Overview of the Joint Duty Program

The Office of the Director of National Intelligence (ODNI) directive for the Joint Duty Program[1] requires that Intelligence Community (IC) personnel participating in the Joint Duty Program rotate from their employing or home element to a joint duty position in another IC element (the gaining element) for at least 12 months and for no more than 36 months, unless a written exception for a different time frame has been requested and approved.[2] Joint duty positions are normally classified at a pay grade of at least General Schedule grade 13 or equivalent. The ODNI policy guidance[3] for the Joint Duty Program further states that, by successfully completing an assignment to a gaining agency and the IC Joint Leadership Development Program (a training program designated for Joint Duty Program participants), individuals receive the "joint duty certification" they will need to apply for promotion to senior level (above General Schedule grade 15 or equivalent) positions.[4]

Under the policy guidance, participating individuals can receive joint duty credit for working

- in another IC element,
- in ODNI or one of its components,[5]
- within a home agency in a position that has been specifically designated as providing joint duty credit,

[1]Intelligence Community Directive 601, *Human Capital: Joint Intelligence Community Duty Assignments* (May 16, 2006) (as amended Sept. 4, 2009).

[2]A joint duty assignment may also be a permanent assignment of an employee from a position in one IC element to a position in another IC element.

[3]Intelligence Community Policy Guidance 601.1, *Intelligence Community Civilian Joint Duty Program Implementing Instructions* (June 25, 2007) (as amended Sept. 4, 2009).

[4]Exemptions to the joint duty certification requirement can be granted if a senior position is unique and requires expertise that cannot be found elsewhere.

[5]The ODNI components include organizations such as the National Counterterrorism Center, the National Counterproliferation Center, and the National Counterintelligence Executive.

- in certain liaison and equivalent positions or on internal assignments (e.g., serving on joint task forces), and
- in an organization outside the IC.[6]

In addition, individuals may request joint duty credit for certain assignments that they previously completed inside or outside the IC. Furthermore, any individual deployed to a designated combat zone for 179 days or more will satisfy the 12-month minimum requirement for joint duty credit.

ODNI established the Joint Duty Program website where the IC elements are to post opportunities (vacancy announcements) for joint duty positions that the agencies wish to fill on a rotational basis. Each IC element is responsible for posting all joint duty opportunities available on the ODNI Joint Duty website. The corresponding vacancy announcements are to include pertinent information about the position, such as qualification requirements, duty location, time frame, and security clearance requirements. ODNI officials explained that announcements may be posted on a classified and unclassified version of the website. Each IC element has designated a point of contact who is responsible for coordinating the individual joint duty assignments of its program participants. In addition, individuals apply for joint duty assignments using the internal policies and procedures established by their home IC element. A proposed joint duty assignment must be approved by the employee's first-level supervisor and second-level manager. Further, ODNI has developed a standard memorandum of understanding that includes provisions governing rotational assignments and is used by all of the IC elements, who then tailor the provisions to govern each individual rotational assignment.

While on a joint duty assignment, an individual generally remains a permanent employee of his or her home agency. The person designated as that individual's immediate supervisor at the gaining agency evaluates the individual's performance during the joint duty assignment period. A higher level management official at the gaining agency reviews the evaluation and provides it to a designated official from the individual's

---

[6]This could include organizations such as the National Security Council, the Homeland Security Council, the President's Intelligence Advisory Board, and other comparable interagency, intergovernmental, private sector, non-governmental, academic or educational, foreign national, or international organizations.

home agency, who then comments on the evaluation in writing and submits this for inclusion in the final performance evaluation provided to the employee. The individual's rating is determined using the home agency's performance management system and associated forms. The gaining agency determines whether the individual receives a performance bonus and funds any bonus awarded. After completion of a joint duty assignment, the home agency is responsible for placing an individual in his or her former (or an equivalent) position and duty location, unless other provisions are agreed to by the employee. Claims for joint duty credit must be filed by employees on a standard form that is available on the ODNI Joint Duty Program website. Employees submit the claim forms to their employing IC element in accordance with the internal policies and processes of that agency, along with official documentation of the claimed assignment.

Appendix IV: Comments from the Department of Homeland Security

U.S. Department of Homeland Security
Washington, DC 20528

Homeland Security

June 14, 2012

Brenda S. Farrell
Director, Defense Capabilities and Management
U.S. Government Accountability Office
441 G Street, NW
Washington, DC 20548

Re: Draft Report GAO-12-679, "INTELLIGENCE COMMUNITY PERSONNEL: Strategic
Approach and Training Requirements Needed to Guide Joint Duty Program"

Dear Ms. Farrell,

Thank you for the opportunity to review and comment on this draft report. The U.S. Department of Homeland Security (DHS) appreciates the U.S. Government Accountability Office's (GAO's) work in planning and conducting its review and issuing this report.

DHS and U.S. Coast Guard (USCG) senior leadership recognizes how critically important it is that all components of the U.S. intelligence community (IC) operate in an effective and collaborative manner. This includes ensuring that civilian intelligence leaders understand the scope and complexity of the IC and are able to integrate and engage the IC's vast resources in support of our national security mission.

The draft report contained one recommendation directed to the USCG and with which DHS concurs. Specifically, GAO recommended that the Commandant of the U.S. Coast Guard:

Recommendation: Take steps to participate in the Joint Duty Program consistent with ODNI policy and guidance.

Response: Concur. Establishing a formal IC Civilian Joint Duty Program (JDP) is one of the USCG's many human resource priorities and one for which policy and guidance is presently being developed. The Coast Guard Intelligence civilian workforce comprises an important but small percentage of the USCG's intelligence enterprise, and only a small portion of that workforce meets the criteria of Intelligence Community Directive (ICD)-601, *Human Capital Joint Intelligence Community Duty Assignments*.

From a macro Joint Duty perspective, Coast Guard Intelligence has approximately 100 intelligence billets assigned to other agencies (including many in the IC) to leverage interagency resources and capabilities, as well as provide substantive USCG maritime expertise to our partners. However, since USCG is a military organization, the majority of these billets are military vice civilian ones, and as such they do not fall under the scope of ICD 601. We believe these military positions do. however, allow USCG to operate within the spirit of the JDP for information sharing. collaboration. and professional development.

USCG anticipates making significant progress developing its civilian JDP during the coming months as staff is again in place to work this issue. Specifically, the strategic workforce staff for Coast Guard Intelligence consists of only three billets. which are all currently vacant. In the interim. a GS-12 employee from elsewhere within the staff has been redirected to focus full time on establishing the mechanics of a JDP. For example. this employee is assessing the elements of ICD-601 against DHS and USCG Human Resource policy to determine the ones which can be implemented in the near term. and those requiring additional policy review and/or development to facilitate a robust JDP. The employee will also coordinate and collaborate with DHS Intelligence & Analysis. also a member of the IC. which has been working to further develop and refine its JDP to determine those aspects which can be incorporated into the USCG's new program.

Again. thank you for the opportunity to review and comment on this draft report. Please feel free to contact me if you have any questions. We look forward to working with you in the future.

Sincerely.

Jim H. Crumpacker
Director
Departmental GAO-OIG Liaison Office

2

Appendix V: Comments from the Office of the Director of National Intelligence

JUN 1 1 2012

Ms. Brenda S. Farrell
Director
Defense Capabilities and Management
United States Government Accountability Office
Washington, DC 20548

Dear Ms. Farrell,

The Office of the Director of National Intelligence (ODNI) appreciates the opportunity to respond to the Government Accountability Office's (GAO) draft report (GAO-12-679) *"Intelligence Community Personnel: Strategic Approach and Training Requirements Needed to Guide Joint Duty Program."*

Regarding GAO's formal recommendations, we understand Coast Guard Intelligence has been asked to provide formal comment on Recommendation 1 (US Coast Guard takes steps to participate in Joint Duty); therefore, we defer to the Coast Guard's response with regard to Recommendation 1. The ODNI concurs with Recommendation 2 (ODNI develop a strategic framework to implement the program) and partially concurs with Recommendation 3 (ODNI develop and document the programs training requirement and develop a plan and timeline for implementing them). The first enclosure provides the ODNI response to GAO's findings and recommendations and the second enclosure provides the technical edits

Should you have any questions please contact the Office of Legislative Affairs at (703) 275-2473.

Kathleen Turner
Director of Legislative Affairs

Attachments:

1. ODNI Response to GAO Draft Recommendations (GAO 12-679)
2. ODNI Technical Edits

ODNI Response to Findings and Recommendations in GAO's Draft Report
Intelligence Community Personnel: Strategic Approach and Training Requirements Needed to Guide Joint Duty Program

GAO Finding: "The ODNI has not established specific performance goals or quantifiable metrics for measuring progress of the Joint Duty Program."

ODNI Response: This statement is factually inaccurate.

From its inception the critical performance goal for the IC Civilian Joint Duty Program was that all IC officers earn Joint Duty Credit prior to promotion above GS-15. This requirement was phased in and fully implemented by October 2010. As of our last data call in the Fall of 2011, all but one senior within the IC had been promoted in compliance with Intelligence Community Directive (ICD) 601, "Human Capital, Joint Intelligence Community Duty Assignments." Additionally we collect data to measure the total population of IC personnel with Joint Duty credit to ensure we are consistently developing an increasing cadre of IC officers with Joint Duty experience. These performance measures have been in place since 2007 and were the basis for the 2008 Innovations in American Government Award which was presented to the Joint Duty Program by the Ash Institute for Democratic Governance and Innovation at the Harvard University Kennedy School of Government.

Further, the Director of National Intelligence (DNI) has recognized the success the community has had in meeting this critical performance goal and determined that the Joint Duty Program is sufficiently mature and established within the IC enterprise and therefore capable of being expanded to ensure that intelligence officers have greater access to Joint Duty opportunities earlier in their careers. Thus, the DNI has requested that the Assistant Director of National Intelligence for Human Capital draft a new policy that will allow the Joint Duty Program to move beyond its initial goal of developing IC Leaders with joint perspectives towards developing an integrated IC enterprise at all levels.

GAO Finding: "Absent a comprehensive strategic framework that transcends turnover in program leadership, program efforts are disjointed, and decision makers within ODNI lack the information they need to successfully manage the program."

ODNI Response: We disagree with this statement and find no evidence in the GAO report to substantiate this claim.

The Joint Duty Program has developed significantly in the six years since its inception and is a key tool to assist in the integration of the IC. As stated above, the IC Joint Duty Program has met the critical performance measures identified and implemented by ICD 601. While we agree that the program could benefit from a single comprehensive strategic document, we disagree that the program cannot be, and has not been successful without such a document.

GAO Recommendation 1: To help ensure that the personnel in all of the Intelligence Community (IC) elements fully understand the U.S. Coast Guard's intelligence mission to secure the nation's ports and coastal waters, that the Coast Guard's civilian intelligence employees do not miss an opportunity to develop collaborative relationships with and to understand other IC elements, and that U.S. Coast Guard civilians remain viable for promotions to senior positions requiring joint duty credit, we recommend that the Commandant of the U.S. Coast Guard take steps to participate in the Joint Duty Program consistent with ODNI Policy and Guidance.

ODNI Response: ODNI defers to the U.S. Coast Guard to provide a formal response to this recommendation.

GAO Recommendation 2: To improve the effectiveness of the implementation of the Joint Duty Program and to help ensure that institutional knowledge about the program transcends the individual tenure of each serving Joint Duty Program Chief, we recommend that the Director of National Intelligence (DNI) develop a comprehensive strategic framework for the Joint Duty Program. This framework could include such items as:

- Clearly defining its mission;
- Establishing performance goals;
- Developing quantifiable metrics for measuring progress toward achieving performance goals;
- Determining the financial resources necessary to accomplish the mission of the program;
- Using performance information and metrics to make decisions to improve the program; and
- Communicating results effectively with each of the IC elements.

ODNI Response: ODNI concurs with this recommendation.

We concur that the IC Civilian Joint Duty Program would benefit from a single comprehensive strategic document and the DNI has requested that a program strategy be developed in conjunction with the ongoing Joint Duty policy revision to help guide the program. The DNI appreciates GAOs guidance and suggestions on what such a strategy should include and will give them due consideration as a strategy is developed and implemented.

GAO Recommendation 3: To fully comply with the requirements of IRTPA and facilitate the widest possible understanding and collaboration among the IC, we recommend that the DNI:

- Establish formal training and education requirements for the Joint Duty Program, revise the existing policy guidance to clearly identify and describe these requirements, and eliminate the waiver that is presently in guidance; and
- Develop a formal plan and timeline to implement the training and education component of the Joint Duty Program.

ODNI Response: ODNI partially concurs with this recommendation.

We concur that the ODNI needs to provide the Intelligence Community formal guidance regarding the learning component to the Joint Duty Program. The ADNI/HC will develop this guidance in conjunction with the revision of the Joint Duty Policy. However, the ODNI does not concur with the GAO's assertion that the current program is not fully complying with the requirements of IRTPA, which states only that the Program "*may* include ... the establishment of requirements for education, training, service, and evaluation for service involving more than one element of the intelligence community." **Section 102A(I)((3)(B) of the National Security Act of 1947, as amended by Section 1011 of the Intelligence Reform and Terrorism Prevention Act of 2004.**

Appendix VI: GAO Contact and Staff Acknowledgments

GAO Contact	Brenda S. Farrell, (202) 512-3604 or farrellb@gao.gov
Staff Acknowledgments	In addition to the contact named above, David Moser (Assistant Director), Patrick Breiding, Renee Brown, Mae Jones, James Krustapentus, Gregory Marchand, Steven Putansu, Jillena Roberts, Amie Steele, and John Van Schaik made key contributions to this report.

GAO's Mission	The Government Accountability Office, the audit, evaluation, and investigative arm of Congress, exists to support Congress in meeting its constitutional responsibilities and to help improve the performance and accountability of the federal government for the American people. GAO examines the use of public funds; evaluates federal programs and policies; and provides analyses, recommendations, and other assistance to help Congress make informed oversight, policy, and funding decisions. GAO's commitment to good government is reflected in its core values of accountability, integrity, and reliability.
Obtaining Copies of GAO Reports and Testimony	The fastest and easiest way to obtain copies of GAO documents at no cost is through GAO's website (www.gao.gov). Each weekday afternoon, GAO posts on its website newly released reports, testimony, and correspondence. To have GAO e-mail you a list of newly posted products, go to www.gao.gov and select "E-mail Updates."
Order by Phone	The price of each GAO publication reflects GAO's actual cost of production and distribution and depends on the number of pages in the publication and whether the publication is printed in color or black and white. Pricing and ordering information is posted on GAO's website, http://www.gao.gov/ordering.htm. Place orders by calling (202) 512-6000, toll free (866) 801-7077, or TDD (202) 512-2537. Orders may be paid for using American Express, Discover Card, MasterCard, Visa, check, or money order. Call for additional information.
Connect with GAO	Connect with GAO on Facebook, Flickr, Twitter, and YouTube. Subscribe to our RSS Feeds or E-mail Updates. Listen to our Podcasts. Visit GAO on the web at www.gao.gov.
To Report Fraud, Waste, and Abuse in Federal Programs	Contact: Website: www.gao.gov/fraudnet/fraudnet.htm E-mail: fraudnet@gao.gov Automated answering system: (800) 424-5454 or (202) 512-7470
Congressional Relations	Katherine Siggerud, Managing Director, siggerudk@gao.gov, (202) 512-4400, U.S. Government Accountability Office, 441 G Street NW, Room 7125, Washington, DC 20548
Public Affairs	Chuck Young, Managing Director, youngc1@gao.gov, (202) 512-4800 U.S. Government Accountability Office, 441 G Street NW, Room 7149 Washington, DC 20548

Please Print on Recycled Paper.

www.ingramcontent.com/pod-product-compliance
Lightning Source LLC
Chambersburg PA
CBHW080914290526
45795CB00007BA/2524